I Need The Light!
Companion
Journal and
Diary

JANET MORRISON

Cover designed by Janet Morrison on Bookbrush.com. Formatted by Janet Morrison using Atticus.io.

Sources Used in This Book and in I Need The Light! 26 Weekly Devotionals to Help You Through Winter

The Acts of the Apostles, by Barclay   William Barclay, *The Acts of the Apostles, Revised Edition* (Westminster John Knox Press, 1976).

Good News Bible   English, Bible. *Today's Good News Bible: The Bible in Today's English Version*, 1976.

The Gospel of Matthew, by Barclay   Barclay, William. *The Gospel of Matthew, Volume One, Revised Edition: Chapters 1-32* (Westminster John Knox Press, 1975).

Halley's Bible Handbook   Henry H. Halley, *Halley's Bible Handbook: An Abbreviated Bible Commentary*, 1964.

The Layman's Bible Commentary, Vol II Isaiah by Wright Wright, B. Ernest. Layman, *Layman's Bible Commentary: Vol II Isaiah*, 1963.

The Layman's Bible Commentary, Vol. 19 John, by Wright Wright, B. Ernest. Layman, *Layman's Bible Commentary: Vol. 19 John*, 1963.

The Letters of James and Peter, by Barclay   Barclay, William. *The Letters of James and Peter, Revised Edition* (Westminster John Knox Press, 1976).

The Letters of John and Jude, by Barclay   Barclay, William. *The Letters of John and Jude, Revised Edition* (Westminster John Knox Press, 1975).

The Letters to the Philippians, Colossians, and Thessalonians, by Barclay   Barclay, William. *The Letters to the Philippians, Colossians, and Thessalonians, Revised Edition* (Westminster John Knox Press, 1975).

The Letters to Timothy, Titus, and Philemon, by Barclay Barclay, William. *The Letters to Timothy, Titus, and Philemon, Revised Edition* (Westminster John Knox Press, 1975).

The Living Bible   Tyndale House Publishers, *The Living Bible, Paraphrased* (Tyndale House Publishers, 1971).

Matthew For Everyone, Part 1   Wright, N.T. *Matthew For Everyone, Part 1* (Westminster John Knox Press, 2002)

The Message   Eugene H. Peterson, *The Message: The Bible in Contemporary Language* (Tyndale House, 2005).

New Oxford Annotated Bible   Oxford University Press et al., *New Oxford Annotated Bible*, 1991.

NIV Study Bible   Zondervan, *NIV Study Bible, Fully Revised Edition* (Zondervan, 2020).

The Psalms of David, in Metre   *The Psalms of David, in Metre* (Philadelphia: William S. Young, 1849).

Reading the Bible with Rabbi Jesus   Lois Tverberg, *Reading the Bible with Rabbi Jesus: How a Jewish Perspective Can Transform Your Understanding (Baker Books, 2018).*

Sitting at the Feet of Rabbi Jesus   Ann Spangler and Lois Tverberg, *Sitting at the Feet of Rabbi Jesus: How the Jewishness of Jesus Can Transform Your Faith. Zondervan, 2018.*

The TouchPoint Bible   Tyndale House Publishers, *The TouchPoint Bible,* 1996.

Walking in the Dust of Rabbi Jesus   Lois Tverberg, *Walking in the Dust of Rabbi Jesus: How the Jewish Words of Jesus Can Change Your Life* (Zondervan, 2012).

Introduction

The Introduction to this companion journal and diary for *I Need The Light! 26 Weekly Devotionals to Help You Through Winter* is almost identical to the Introduction in that devotional book. I am including it here in case someone gets a copy of this journal but does not yet have a copy of the devotional book. It would be possible to use this journal without also having the devotional book, but your experience will be greatly enriched by using the two books together.

Winter has always been my least favorite season. I have had Chronic Fatigue Syndrome (CFS)/Myalgic Encephalomyelitis (ME) since 1987 and Fibromyalgia since soon thereafter. These are year-round conditions, but they are made worse by cold temperatures and sudden changes in the weather.

A few years ago, I was diagnosed with Seasonal Affective Disorder (SAD). My physician's assistant urged me to get outside in the early- to mid-morning to soak in the natural light to ease my SAD symptoms. I have had limited success because I am not a "morning person" and in cool and cold weather I have the added body aches due to CFS/ME and Fibromyalgia.

Fibromyalgia exacerbates my dislike of cold weather. In the autumn and winter months I often wake up in the morning in the fetal position with my fingers curled into my palms. I am stiff all over and have almost constant pain in my neck and head. This pain sometimes permeates into my gums. After 38 years of this illness, it is just a part of the life I have accepted.

I have a lower-than-normal core body temperature. My body, therefore, concentrates its heat around my essential organs. This results in limited heat for my hands and feet. They are cold for six months of the year.

I do not seek your sympathy for any of these maladies. I mention them in this introduction merely to explain what my experience has been and to let others who suffer with any of these issues know that they are not alone.

Everybody has something. Illness and mental challenges are a part of life. Jesus never promised us a life without pain, sorrow, grief, or frustration. He promised to be here with us.

The devotional book that this journal is a companion to grew out of my experience.

As I walked one cold morning, I had to will my feet to keep stepping forward. In an effort to get into a rhythm and remind myself why I was walking on such a cold day, I repeated over and over the words, "I need the light. I need the light." It was on around the fifth repetition that "light" (lowercase) became "Light" (capitalized.)

I needed sunlight on my face to combat the seasonal tendency I have not to be joyful in the fall and winter months. The light my face needs for SAD is the lowercase "light." The capitalized "Light" my soul — my whole being — needs is Jesus Christ.

I had the idea to write a book highlighting some of the times and ways in which "light" and "Light" appear in the Bible to illustrate my need for both light and Light. It was as I was studying Matthew 5:14-16 that a "lightbulb" came on in my head and I realized there is a third part to the equation: God has given me an assignment. I am to be a light to the world!

I need sunlight in the mornings to overcome SAD.

I need the Lord Jesus Christ in all aspects of my being because He is my Rock. He is my Salvation. He overcame death for me. He overcame death for you.

I need to be light — to be a light — to shine God's Light for others to see, to reflect His Light and not keep Him a secret.

God has made me a light-bearer. He has put me on a hilltop and a light stand and He expects me to be generous with His Light.

I have no formal religious training. I grew up in the Presbyterian denomination and am a member of a congregation affiliated with the Presbyterian Church, USA. I have written this devotional book as a layperson.

I am not an "in your face" kind of Christian, so I stepped out of my comfort zone to write the devotional book. If you are looking for a book that scares you into being a Christian, it and this journal are not for you.

You might prefer to read versions of the Bible that I have not included in this book. You might not agree with all my statements or all the statements I have quoted from other sources.

I selected 26 Scripture passages about light or The Light. After studying those passages in five versions of the Bible, I arranged them in the order that made sense to me and decided to present them as 26 weekly devotionals.

Winter is not 26 weeks long but, if you are like me, your Seasonal Affective Disorder or increased pain from fibromyalgia sets in around the first of September here in the northern hemisphere and hangs on until the daytime temperatures reach the 70s F. That is about 26 weeks, or half the year.

Some of the weekly devotionals include a section called "My Thoughts." Those are the weeks that the Scripture passage either especially spoke to me or sparked questions or deeper thinking in my mind. Each devotional includes a sentence to remember, a thought pattern interrupter to help you combat negative thoughts, a suggested activity, and a recipe for a dish I find comforting. Most of the devotionals include insights from commentaries written by Rev. William Barclay.

Rev. William Barclay was a Presbyterian minister in Scotland. He wrote a series of commentaries covering the entire Protestant Bible. My mother relied heavily on Barclay's books and H.H. Halley's book, *Halley's Bible Handbook* as she taught Bible lessons and Sunday School for many years. I inherited her reliance on those resources.

The thought pattern interrupters are suggested for you to consider to counteract any negative thoughts you are having due to the season.

The recipes are some of my favorite cold weather foods. They all fall into the category of "comfort foods." I hope you will find comfort and warmth in the ones you choose to make.

It is my prayer that whether or not you have Seasonal Affective Disorder or physical conditions that make the cooler months of the year challenging, that you will find these 26 devotionals helpful in your daily journey.

Janet Morrison

Contents

Let There Be Light

T he Scripture for this week is Genesis 1:1-5.

Which version of this Scripture spoke to you? How did it affect you?

What jumped out at you?

Did one of these versions of Genesis 1:1-5 give you new insight? Write about that.

Have you ever experienced a "Land of the Midnight Sun" situation? If so, was it disorienting to have a vastly different number of hours of light or darkness than you were accustomed to?

How are you using this week's Thought Pattern Interrupter? Did you write it down and post it where you will see it throughout the week? Is it helping you? How is it helping you?

Is there a suggested activity in this week's devotional that you want to pursue? Write down how and when you plan to do it.

Do you know someone who might benefit from reading this devotional?

Did you make Mama's Drop Biscuits? How did they turn out? Will you make them again?

Notes:

A Lamp to My Feet

The Scripture for this week is Psalm 119:105.

Which version of this Scripture spoke to you? How did it affect you?

What jumped out at you?

Did one of these versions of Psalm 119:105 give you new insight? Write about that.

Did Lois Tverberg's explanation of "law" and "guidance" or "teaching" help you to see the "laws" in the Old Testament in a new light?

List some reasons you think God created winter.

How are you using this week's Thought Pattern Interrupter? Did you write it down and post it where you will see it throughout the week? Is it helping you? How is it helping you?

Do you know someone who might benefit from reading this devotional?

Did you give some thought to donating any of your fall or winter clothes to a thrift shop or homeless shelter? If so, make a plan and set a date to do it. If you carried out that plan, how did it make you feel?

Did you make Mary Jane's Meatloaf? How did it turn out? Did you like it? Did you divide and freeze it to enjoy later?

Notes:

The People Will See a Great Light

T he Scripture for this week is Isaiah 9:1-2.

Which version of this Scripture spoke to you? How did it affect you?

What jumped out at you?

Did one of these versions of Isaiah 9:1-2 give you new insight? Write about that.

Does having the conflict between Israel and Gaza in mind make you think differently about this week's Scripture?

How are you using this week's Thought Pattern Interrupter? Did you write it down and post it where you will see it throughout the week? Is it helping you? How is it helping you?

Did you do this week's suggested activity? Did you clean out a closet? If so, good for you! It is a daunting task. If you set aside some item to donate, have you made a plan to accomplish that?

Do you know someone who might benefit from reading this devotional?

Did you make Barbecue Stacks? Is this a new way for you to enjoy barbecue? Will you make this recipe again?

Notes:

John the Baptist

T he Scripture for this week is John 1:6-8.

Which version of this Scripture spoke to you? How did it affect you?

What jumped out at you?

Did one of these versions of John 1:6-8 give you new insight about John the Baptist? Write about that.

Did the information from *The Gospel of John, Vol. 1,* by William Barclay give you new insight into John the Baptist?

Do you feel called to bear witness to Jesus Christ?

How are you using this week's Thought Pattern Interrupter? Did you write it down and post it where you will see it throughout the week? Is it helping you? How is it helping you? Think of a blessing of winter that you will try to embrace. Write it down. Can you think of more than one blessing of winter?

Did you get to do any part of this week's suggested activity? I hope you got to share a meal with a friend.

Do you know someone who might benefit from reading this devotional?

Did you make Easy Cheesy Lasagna? Will you make this recipe again?

Notes:

Jesus is The Real Thing

T he Scripture for this week is John 1:9.

Which version of this Scripture spoke to you? How did it affect you?

What jumped out at you?

Did one of these versions of John 1:9 give you new insight? Write about that.

Had you ever thought about Jesus Christ as "underived" or real light, like the sun? You are to reflect Jesus' Light, just as the moon reflects the sun's light.

Do you feel called to cast a light on Jesus? (You don't have to use the extreme tactics used by John the Baptist.)

The next time you experience a nighttime thunderstorm, do not fear. Rather, stop and think how that flash of lightning is like how Jesus Christ shines a light to guide you. He did not come to frighten you, but to guide you and to remove your shadows of doubt.

What do you fear? Sickness? Pain? Suffering? Winter? Death? Jesus Christ will be with you through sickness, pain, suffering, this winter, and even death. It is normal to fear or dread sickness and suffering. Many of us dread winter. But if you accept Jesus Christ as your Lord and Savior, you never have to fear death. Write down your fears and the things you dread. Talk to God about them.

How are you using this week's Thought Pattern Interrupter? Did you write it down and post it where you will see it throughout the week? Is it helping you? How is it helping you? What is weighing on your mind this week? Are you grappling with a major decision? A life-changing decision? Do you have to give someone bad news? Are you expecting bad news from your doctor, a loved one, or your supervisor? Whatever it is that has you baffled or worried, give it to God in prayer. Ask God to help you with whatever it is that has you distracted, worried, uneasy, or even frightened this week.

Sometimes it helps to put your thoughts or prayers in writing. Take time to do that today and see if it helps you to organize your thoughts. See if it helps you to get to the root of your current worry or concern.

If you seek God's guidance, He will help you. And after you make your decision, don't second guess yourself. You did the best you could at the time with the information you had.

Did one of this week's suggested activities appeal to you? Did you accomplish it or make a plan to do it? After you have done that activity, write down how it made you feel to help someone.

Do you know someone who might benefit from reading this devotional?

Did you make Aunt Della's Chicken and Rice Casserole? I hope you like it as much as I do! Will you make it again?

Notes:

The People Will See a Great Light

T he Scripture for this week is Matthew 4:12-17.

Were you aware that the Greek word in the original text means "tested" instead of "tempted"? That was reassuring to me. I don't believe God tempts us. He might test us, like He tested Jesus in the wilderness, but I don't believe He tempts us to do wrong. What do you think? Has this week's devotional prompted you to question what you believe about what is traditionally called "the temptation of Jesus"?

Did the information from *The Gospel of Matthew, Vol. 1, Revised Edition,* by William Barclay give you a new perspective on the population of the district of Galilee when Jesus walked on Earth in human form?

Which version of this week's Scripture spoke to you?

What jumped out at you?

Did one of these versions of Matthew 4:12-17 give you new insight?

In Matthew 4:12-17, Jesus stepped out of His comfort zone to begin His ministry. Is God calling you to step out of your comfort zone?

Did you do something this week to lift your spirits?

Do you know someone who might benefit from reading this devotional?

Did you make Slow Cooker Blackeyed Pea Stew? Did you freeze servings to enjoy later? It is nice to be able to pull a container of soup or stew out of the freezer when you don't feel like cooking!

Notes:

Y'all Are the Light of the World

The Scripture for this week is Matthew 5:13-16.

What was your initial reaction to the title of this week's devotional? Were you amused? Were you intrigued? Do you have a better understanding of the American Southerners' use of "y'all" than you did before reading the introduction to this week's devotional?

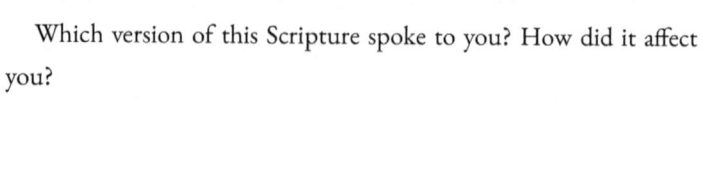

Which version of this Scripture spoke to you? How did it affect you?

What jumped out at you?

Did one of these versions of Matthew 5:13-16 give you new insight? Write about that.

Do you think Jesus was saying we as individuals are to be the light of the world or Christians as a group? Or both?

Are you gaining a deeper understanding of your responsibility as a Christian to be a light to show others the way?

William Barclay indicated that Christians should have the courage to go first, to speak up against injustice, to warn people out of a place of love and not anger. Have you ever found yourself in such a situation?

How much courage did it take for you to speak up or act?

Is this something you often feel called to do?

How have people reacted to you when you have spoken up against an injustice?

Did your family and friends support you, or ridicule you?

Does it get any easier to be that first person to speak up or do you find it more difficult now to "stand on your own two feet" and risk making yourself a target?

What is happening in your community, state, or nation at the present time that you feel like you need to speak up about?

Have you spoken up about it yet? Will you? If not, what is stopping you?

Do you have a better understanding now about the difference between "the people of Israel" of the Bible and the political State of Israel of today?

Do you think a person can be anti-Israel and not be anti-Semitic? Is this a difficult matter for you? Next week's devotional touches on this again. It is a concept that is misunderstood by many people because they don't know the history of the formation of the State of Israel.

Do you see yourself as a child of God? Do you see every person in the world as a child of God and just as important in God's eyes as you are?

Have you identified an item you have or could purchase that you could donate to a homeless shelter?

Can you think of someone who would benefit from reading this week's devotional?

Have you made Easy No-Egg Cornbread? Did you have any leftovers for the next day or to freeze for later? Will you make it again?

Notes:

He is a Light to Reveal God to the Nations

The Scripture for this week is Luke 2:32.

Last week's devotional touched on the difference between "the people of Israel" of the Bible and the political State of Israel of today. This week's devotional introduction brought that up again. Do you have a better understanding now about the difference between "the people of Israel" of the Bible and the political State of Israel of today? Do you think a person can be anti-Israel and not be anti-Semitic? Is this a difficult matter for you?

Which version of this Scripture spoke to you? How did it affect you?

What jumped out at you?

Did one of these versions of Luke 2:32 give you new insight? Write about that.

Before reading this week's devotional, had you ever tried to put yourself in Simeon's place and time?

What do you think the other people at the temple that day thought when they heard Simeon announce that Mary and Joseph's infant son was the Messiah? If you had been there, do you think you would have believed Simeon, or would you have thought he was crazy or had dementia?

Has this week's Thought Pattern Interrupter helped you? How have you used it? Have you found something good in each day, even though it is winter and you cannot get warm?

Sunday

Monday

Tuesday

Wednesday

Thursday

Friday

Saturday

Have you visited a friend in person or by phone this week? If not, maybe you can do that next week.

Do you know someone who might benefit from reading this week's devotional?

Have you made Marie's Cereal Mix? If you find it addictive, just remember it is a much healthier version than the traditional recipe. Consider making it again and sharing part of it with a friend or neighbor.

Notes:

Your Body Fills with Light

The Scripture for this week is Matthew 6:22-23.

Did the "Setting the Stage" introduction to this week's devotional give you a clearer understanding of terms such as "the evil eye" and "a good eye" as explained by Lois Tverberg in *Walking in the Dust of Rabbi Jesus: How the Jewish Words of Jesus Can Change Your Life*? Were you surprised to learn that in the parlance of the Jews, "your 'eye' is really about your attitude toward money"?

What does your relationship with money say about your relationship with God?

Which version of this Scripture spoke to you? How did it affect you?

What jumped out at you?

Did one of these versions of Matthew 6:22-23 give you new insight? Write about that.

Did you find the imagery in this week's Scripture in *The Message* gave you some new pictures in your mind of what it means for your eyes to be "the windows into your body"?

William Barclay's thoughts about Matthew 6:22-23 in *The Gospel of Matthew, Volume 1, Revised Edition*, focused on the spiritual state of the eye. Barclay listed things that can distort our spiritual vision: prejudice, jealousy, and self-conceit. We're all guilty of each of those at various times in our lives. Only Jesus Christ is perfect. Do you struggle with any of those three examples? If so, ask God to help you make a plan to try to do better.

Had you considered Matthew 6:22-23 in terms of generosity? Barclay writes about a generous spirit and an ungenerous spirit. Do you have a generous spirit? Do you keep a generous spirit when you are tempted to judge others?

Review the keywords found in the five versions of Matthew 6:22-23: light, lamp, window, eye, pure, evil, greed, distrust, squinty-eyed, musty cellar, sound eyes, eyes that are no good, healthy eye, unhealthy eye, sunshine into the soul, plunges into darkness, prejudice, jealousy, and self-conceit. Could you have imagined so many images would be found in five versions of just two Bible verses? Which of these words will stay with you and come to mind the next time you read or hear Matthew 6:22-23?

Is there a Ronald McDonald House or other such facility in your city that you can contact? Ask what they need that you or a group you are in can give? It might be something physical. It might be your time that they need. They might just want you to spread the word about what they do and what they need. Don't feel bad if you are not physically or financially able to help them. All of us can pray for the children and families they serve. Perhaps you know someone or a group or organization that can.

Do you know someone who might benefit from reading this week's devotional?

Have you made Presbyterian Hospital Chili? It is a forgiving recipe that you can adjust to your own tastes. It is a wonderful recipe to divide in portions to freeze for later use.

Notes:

No One Lights a Lamp then Hides It

T he Scripture for this week is Luke 8:16-18.

Have you ever been a "miser of what you hear" as we read in Luke 8:16 in *The Message*? If it is gossip we hear, we would be wise to be misers; however, if it is the Word of God that we hear, then we should not be misers and keep what we hear to ourselves. The analogy Jesus makes is that no one lights a lamp and then hides it. Have you ever been a "miser" with the Word of God?

When someone shares gossip with you, what do you do with it?

Verse 18 in this week's Scripture is a warning, but I found it confusing until I read it in *TouchPoint Bible*. Did that version help you understand verse 18?

Which version of Luke 8:16-18 spoke to you?

What jumped out at you?

Did William Barclay's explanation in *The Gospel of Luke, Revised Edition* clarify this Scripture for you?

I find it very hard to ask for help. Just ask my sister! She is constantly telling me that I should ask for help. Is it difficult for you to ask for help?

What kinds of things do you need help with? What is the hardest thing for you to ask for help with?

Did you do this week's suggested activity? How did it go? Did you and your neighbor both enjoy your get-together? What did you serve? Did you get better acquainted? Will you do this again?

Do you know someone who might benefit from reading this week's devotional? What about that neighbor you invited over for coffee, tea, or hot chocolate? What about that person who often shares unwanted gossip?

Have you made Savory Ham and Rice? One way to speed up prep time is to have four cups of cooked rice prepared and frozen or refrigerated in advance and to have the ham sliced in advanced or purchase a package of cubed ham. Do you think you will make this recipe again?

Notes:

It Bears Repeating, No One Lights a Lamp then Hides It

T he Scripture for this week is Luke 11:33-36

Why do you think this lesson is being repeated? Just because it appears in another chapter of Luke? Sometimes we need to look for nuances in the way the same story or parable is presented in different places in the Bible.

This week's Scripture starts out exactly like last week's, but then it goes in a different direction. Were you surprised when this Scripture went from talking about lamps and started talking about our eyes? If this part about our eyes sounds familiar, it is because we studied it in Week 9 in Matthew 6:22-23. The wording in *The Message* used the term "squinty-eyed" and "musty smells" and here we find those words again in Luke 11:33-36.

Which version of Luke 11:33-36 do you prefer? Why?

What jumped out at you, even though this is the third consecutive week we have read at least parts of this story?

Did William Barclay's words from *The Gospel of Luke, Revised Edition* clarify this week's Scripture for you?

Were you touched by Barclay's story of the little girl's reaction to hearing that Jesus was crucified? Does that story make you realize that you have heard the Crucifixion story so many times that you don't really listen now? On Good Friday next spring, try to listen to the story as if you've never heard it before so you can be shocked when you hear the word "crucified."

Have you made a conscious effort this week to let Jesus' Light shine through your face and your actions?

Did you make a list of the things you are thankful for? Repeat it here and on the next page, or write it here and on the next page for the first time.

Do you know someone who would benefit from reading this week's devotional?

Have you make Mexican One Dish? Will you make it again?

Notes:

Parable of the Lost Coin

T he Scripture for this week is Luke 15:8-10.

Which version of this Scripture spoke to you? How did it affect you?

You have, no doubt, heard the Parable of the Lost Coin many times, but what jumped out at you this time?

Did one of these versions of Luke 15:8-10 give you new insight? Write about that.

Until reading the thoughts shared from *The Gospel of Luke, Revised Edition*, by William Barclay, had you considered how dark it would have been in that Palestinian peasant's house or that the dirt floor would have been covered with dried reeds and rushes?

Try to put yourself in the place of the Jews who were hearing this parable for the first time. Their concept of God was not the same as a 21st century Christian's concept of God. The Jews listening to Jesus had never thought of God as a heavenly Father who seeks us even more intensely than the woman in the parable was desperate to find her lost coin.

I had never paid any attention to the mention of light in verse 8 in The Parable of the Lost Coin. Had you? What are your thoughts about God's reason for sending Jesus Christ to us? Reread the last paragraph in the "My Thoughts" section in this week's devotional.

Has this week's Thought Pattern Interrupter helped you? Have you had to remind yourself more than once this week that you are doing the best you can?

An interesting thing happened to me the day before I was writing the journal/diary questions for this week. I received a letter from a dear friend with whom I had lost touch for more than a decade. It turned out that each of us had misinterpreted something the other said the last time we spoke. It also turned out that each of us had regretted the loss of our friendship, thought about the other one many times over the years, but never picked up the phone or written a note to the other one. Thinking back over when I wrote the activity suggestion for this week's devotional, I believe I subconsciously had this particular friend in mind.

For me to receive a thoughtful, sincere, apologetic letter from her the day before I was writing the words you are now reading is nothing short of "a God thing." But it was my friend, who does not have as strong a faith in God as I claim to have who picked up a pen and paper and handwrote a letter to me. I should have been the one writing to apologize to her!

I am still a work in progress. God is still trying to nudge me into being the person who He wants me to be.

I wrote my friend last night. We have now patched things up and renewed our friendship. We were able to pick back up where we left off, which is an indication of a true friendship.

This week, did you write a letter to someone you don't want to lose touch with or someone you need to apologize to? Do it. What do you have to lose? Write down the name of someone you need to write a letter to. If the only way you have to write them is via text, text them; however, if you have their mailing address, write them a letter. There is something special about a letter, especially one that is handwritten. Do it. Write down some notes here to get your thoughts organized for writing that letter.

Do you know someone who might benefit from reading this devotional?

Have you tried the Spoonburgers recipe? Was it a big hit? Will you make it again?

Notes:

The Word was the Source of Life and This Life Brought Light to Mankind

T he Scripture for this week is John 1:4.

Which version of this Scripture spoke to you? How did it affect you?

Was Jesus being called "The Word" a new concept for you. Perhaps it has been a while since you read the first chapter of The Gospel of John and the "Setting the Stage" section of this week's devotional served as a reminder of that for you. Was there anything in "Setting the Stage" that jumped out at you as a new perspective?

Did one of these versions of John 1:4 give you new insight? Write about that.

Did the quote from *Halley's Bible Handbook*, by Henry H. Halley give you something new to think about when you hear the words, "Jesus the Light of the World" now?

I was amazed to find that William Barclay wrote four pages about John 1:4 in his commentary, *The Gospel of John, Vol I, Revised Edition.* He wrote about some of the things John has to say about life. He mentioned that our belief in Jesus has to be more than an intellectual belief. He talked about taking Jesus at His word. He wrote about John the Baptist's purpose. He wrote about three things that stood out to him about Jesus' Light. It is a lot to digest. Of all that Barclay had to say in connection to John 1:4, what made the biggest impression on you?

I have trouble believing that I am good enough. Did you find this week's Thought Pattern Interrupter helpful? Have you had to remind yourself more than once this week that you are good enough? In which areas of life do you sometimes feel like you are not good enough?

Do you know someone struggling with self-worth who might benefit from reading this devotional?

Did this week's activity suggestion prompt you to volunteer at your local animal shelter, if that is permitted? Did it prompt you to think of somewhere else you might be able to volunteer when you feel like it?

Have you made Aunt Lila Mae's Chocolate Pie? I hope it turned out well for you, because it really is delicious. Do you think you will make it again?

Notes:

The Life-Light Blazed Out of the Darkness; the Darkness Couldn't Put it Out

T he Scripture for this week is John 1:5.

The term "Life-Light" for Jesus Christ was new to me. Had you heard Him referred to as a Life-Light before?

All five versions of John 1:5 quoted in *I Need The Light! 26 Weekly Devotionals to Help You Through Winter* are similar in wording. What jumps out at you or really catches your attention in this verse?

Until my later years, I did not think much about the darkness or evil in the world. It is only since the terrorist attacks on the United States on September 11, 2001, that I had to dwell on it. I have come to realize that there is much evil in the world, but John 1:5, in just a few words, give me the assurance that the evil in the world has never and will never overcome or defeat Jesus Christ. I cannot imagine a much more comforting verse in the Bible! What are your thoughts?

I have known all my life that Jesus Christ died for my sins approximately 2,000 years ago, and I have known that Christianity has survived all those years, but until I read the commentary presented for John 1:5 by William Barclay in *The Gospel of John, Vol I, Revised Edition*, did I stop and think about the depth of what that verse says. "But there is a power in Jesus that is undefeatable. The darkness can hate him, but it can never get rid of him.... In every generation the light of Christ still shines in spite of the efforts of men to extinguish the flame." Those are amazing statements! What are your thoughts?

The Layman's Bible Commentary, Vol. 19: John takes us a little deeper into the darkness referenced in John 1:5. The author states that the darkness mentioned in this verse "is more than absence of light; it is an active rejection of God's will, a hostile darkness that opposes the working of the divine Light." Does that explanation give you even more pause?

Is this week's Thought Pattern Interrupter helping you? It is a thought — a knowing — that I have tried to remember throughout my adult life.

Do you know someone who might benefit from reading this devotional?

Did you make Beth's Hot Chocolate this week? Is it the best hot chocolate you have ever tasted? I find it addictive, so I try to only make it once every winter. Did you carry out this week's suggested activity to name something or someone you are thankful for as you take each sip of the hot chocolate? If you cannot have Beth's Hot Chocolate, substitute another beverage and still do the activity.

Notes:

People Working and Living in Truth Welcome God-Light

T he Scripture for this week is John 3:19-21.

Did you take time to read the first 21 verses of the third chapter of John? I urge you to do so, if you haven't already done so this week. There is a lot packed into those 21 verses. You are, not doubt familiar with John 3:16, and you've probably read and heard the story of Jesus' encounter with Nicodemus early in the chapter. To read all 21 verses together might give you a new perspective. Did you pick up on something new this week in your reading of John 3:1-21, or specifically from John 3:19-21?

Before reading the "Setting the Stage" section of Week 15 in *I Need The Light! 26 Weekly Devotionals to Help You Through Winter*, had you been aware of the significance of Nicodemus visiting Jesus at night?

What do you think about the use of the words, "This is the crisis we're in" in *The Message*? Had you ever read John 3:19 with a feeling of urgency before? Do you feel the urgency of those words now?

What jumped out at you in John 3:19-21 as presented in *The Living Bible*? Is there a word that jumped out at you?

Do you see a connection between John 3:19-21 and Jesus Christ's commandment that we "love the Lord your God with all your heart and love others as you love yourself" as mentioned in the devotional? What are your thoughts?

Do you see a connection between The Ten Commandments and the message John is trying to get across to us in John 3:19-21? What are your thoughts?

Is there a word that jumps out at you in John 3:19-21 in *The Living Bible*?

What do you think about William Barclay saying that a person who rejects Jesus condemns himself or herself?

Have you been able to find something to laugh about today? Is using that as this week's Thought Pattern Interrupter been helpful for you?

Take time now to write a letter to your younger self. What wisdom would you give your younger self if you could do that? Do you think your younger self would have listened to you?

Have you tried the Black Bean Soup recipe? Will you make it again?
Did you freeze some for later?

Notes:

The Light of the World

This week's Scripture is John 8:12.

What were your initial thoughts when you read the "Setting the Stage" section in Week 16's devotional?

After the adulterous woman was brought into the temple, Jesus went on to ask the scholars and Pharisees he was addressing if they were sinless, but do you wish Jesus had pointed out in stronger language that the woman caught in adultery was not alone when she was caught?

In *Reading the Bible with Rabbi Jesus: How a Jewish Perspective Can Transform Your Understanding*, Lois Tverberg is critical of *the Message* version of the Bible. Were you familiar with *The Message* as a version of the Bible before you started reading *I Need The Light! 26 Weekly Devotionals to Help You Through Winter*?

Do you find *The Message* helpful as a resource in addition to more traditional versions of the Bible? What do you like about *The Message*? What do you not like about *The Message*?

We have the light the sun provides during the day even if the sun is hidden by clouds. We trust at night that the light of the sun will return to our side of the world the next morning. In the 21st century, in most of the world, we can take light provided by electricity for granted. We can benefit from electric lights any time, day or night. How do you think Jesus' original audience in John 8:12 would have understood His words that He was the Light of the World differently or in a different level than we can hear it today due to our access to light twenty-four hours-a-day?

Do you think Jesus was intentionally taking advantage of the Festival of Booths to refer to Himself as "The Light of the World" since there would have been a large crowd and "Great golden lamps" in the temple court?

Until reading William Barclay's commentary on John 8:12 in *The Gospel of John, Vol. 1, Revised Edition,* were you aware the Jewish rabbis had declared that the name of the Messiah was Light and, therefore, they saw Jesus referring to Himself as "The Light of the World" as blasphemous?

Have you found this week's Thought Pattern Interrupter to be helpful?

Have you called a friend or relative this week?

If you made Slow Cooker Chicken Chili, did you like it? Remember, it freezes well. Will you make it again?

Notes:

Those Who Walk in the Dark Don't Know Where They're Going

The Scripture for this week is John 12:35-36.

This week's Scripture takes place shortly before Jesus' crucifixion. He knew His ministry and His time with His disciples was drawing to a close. It had been a rough time. Judas Iscariot criticized Mary Magdalene for anointing Jesus' feet with expensive perfume instead of selling it for a profit. Jesus raised Lazarus from the dead and brought down the wrath of the chief priests on Lazarus for being the reason Jews were leaving Judaism to follow Jesus. More confusion resulted when Jesus told His followers that He would ascend into heaven. That's not what they had been taught at the temple! All this prompted Jesus to speak the words in John 12:35-36. Until I researched the "Setting the Stage" section for this week's devotional, I had not consciously connected the dots to read John 12:35-36 in the context of the events that had recently transpired and the context of Jesus' knowing His days on Earth were numbered? Had you?

In doing the research to write the "Setting the Stage" section of this week's devotional, I did not recall that the chief priests planned to kill Lazarus after Jesus raised him from the dead. It adds an elevated level of drama and suspense to the story! Was this a new detail for you, too?

As I read John 12:35-36, I try to put myself in the place of the people listening to Jesus say the words. Taking the words at face value leaves some room for confusion for me, even after I know that Jesus is The Light. I can't help but think the meaning must have been clearer in the original language, so His audience could understand what He was trying to convey to them. It takes a leap to get from all the language about walking in the light and walking in the dark to grasping that

Jesus was the Light, if you have never been exposed to the idea of Jesus being The Light. Which of the five versions of John 12:35-36 in the devotional book is the easiest for you to understand?

Have you been able to use this week's Thought Pattern Interrupter? What was something beautiful you saw, heard, or realized today? What about yesterday? Keep it up!

Were you able to make muffins or cornbread (or something else) to share with a neighbor of friend? If you did, what did you make? Don't beat yourself up if you didn't. There's always next week!

Speaking of cornbread, did you try the Creamy Cornbread recipe? How did it turn out? Do you think you will make it again? It goes well with Presbyterian Hospital Chili found in Week 9 in the devotional book, Slow Cooker Chicken Chili found in Week 16 in the devotional book, Slower Cooker Blackeyed Pea Stew found in Week 6 in the devotional book, and .... you get the idea!

Notes:

I Came as a Light so No One Who Believes in Me Should Stay in Darkness

T he Scripture for this week is John 12:46.

This week's Scripture is straightforward. According to William Barclay's commentary, *The Gospel of John, Vol. 2, Revised Edition*, this section of the twelfth chapter of John's Gospel contains "Jesus's last words of public teaching." After this, Jesus focused on instructing His disciples. John 12:56 drives home the lessons of the devotionals in *I Need The Light! 26 Weekly Devotionals to Help You Through Winter*: Jesus is The Light of the World, and to live without Jesus in your heart is to walk in darkness. What are your thoughts?

If you go back and read the verses leading up to John 12:56, you will be reminded that Jesus came to save the world, not to condemn the world. Isn't that reassuring? Is that the way you understand Jesus?

Human beings tend to complicate things. It is people who have added some unattainable rules to Jesus's message. Do you see how simple Jesus tried to make it for us?

Do you know someone who might benefit from reading this devotional?

Has this week's Thought Pattern Interrupter been a good reminder for you this week that you are unique?

Did you send a card or a note to someone who lives alone this week?

Did you get to make Brunswick Stew? It feeds a crowd, or freezes well in small containers and tastes wonderful on a cold winter's day!

Notes:

Paul on the Road to Damascus

The Scripture for this week is Acts 9:1-9.

It is important to remember Paul's background and why he was going to Damascus. His conversion on the Road to Damascus was so complete that it prompted his name change. The "Setting the Stage" section of this week's devotional is lengthier than in any other week, so you might want to read it again. Let's look at it a bit at a time. Paul (formerly, Saul) was a Roman citizen, which meant he was privileged. It is interesting to know that in the first century A.D., citizenship was not determined or automatic based on one's nationality. Roman rulers were happy to bestow citizenship on people of high standing who supported Rome's objectives. Saul certainly fell into that category. Since citizenship today is determined by where one is born (although as I write this in the United States in 2025, that is up for political debate), did Saul/Paul being a Roman citizen meant anything to you before reading the "Setting the Stage" section of the devotional for this week?

Before reading the "Setting the Stage" section of the devotional for this week, and William Barclay's commentary from *The Acts of the Apostles, Revised Edition*, were you aware that Saul had gone to the Sanhedrin go obtain official paperwork (essentially, search warrants) so he could hunt down the Christians in Damascus and arrest them? That, of course, is not the point of the story, but it adds a layer of determination in Saul. What are your thoughts?

It is easy to fall into the trap of thinking you know the story of Paul on the Road to Damascus because you have probably read and heard it many times. It is important when you come to a familiar story in the Bible to take time to read it slowly and look for something new. Look for something that surprises you in Acts 9:1-9.

The Scripture tells us that there were men traveling with Saul. Those men heard the voice saying, "Saul, Saul! Why do you persecute me? I am Jesus, the one you are persecuting! Now get up and go into the city and await my further instructions." But the men with Saul saw no one. The New Revised Standard Version of the Bible says the men "stood speechless because they heard the voice but saw no one." It does not say whether they saw the light that blinded Saul. Have you ever thought about what effect the event had on the men with Saul? After the event, they had to lead the blinded Saul into Damascus. Try to imagine if you had been there. Write down your thoughts.

William Barclay's commentary explains that the men with Saul were officers of the Sanhedrin, which makes sense if you stop to think about the fact that Saul was going to Damascus to arrest people. Without reading Barclay's commentary, I had not known that. Had you realized the men with Saul were officers of the Sanhedrin?

There were other points of interest in Barclay's commentary, including the distance between Jerusalem and Damascus, the slapping of Paul by the guards at the Sanhedrin in the twenty-second chapter of Acts, and the significance of Paul calling Ananias, the high priest, "A white-washed wall." Did you remember those details from your earlier readings of the story of Paul on the Road to Damascus? If not, it is perhaps because, like me, you read it or hear it without focus because you have heard it so many times.

Becoming a Christian emboldened Paul to call the members of the Sanhedrin "Brethren" as if he was one of their peers. That resulted in Ananias ordering the guards to slap Paul. That did not silence Paul, though, because he reminded the rulers that striking the cheek of an Israelite was equivalent to striking the glory of God. The Jewish priests on the Sanhedrin would have known Paul when he was Saul. They knew how dedicated he had been in hunting down Jesus's followers. Can you imagine how shocked they were when Saul returned as Paul and had become a fiery advocate for the Christians? Picture that scene!

Have you ever been persecuted for your faith in Jesus Christ? How did you react?

If you were brought before a court and charged with being a Christian, how would you defend yourself?

Is Jesus calling you by name and instructing you to go and He will tell you what to do? Has Jesus been calling you, but you have ignored Him?

What do you think Jesus wants you to do?

Has this week's Thought Pattern Interrupter helped you to hold on to the knowledge that winter won't last forever?

Did you have an opportunity this week to visit a public library and listen to how excited children are to select and check out books?

Did you make Lasagna Soup? Had you had Lasagna Soup before? It makes a lot, but cooked pasta doesn't always freeze well. Enjoy it for several days!

Notes:

Let Light Shine Out of Darkness

T he Scripture for this week is II Corinthians 4:1-6

You, no doubt, noticed that this week's Scripture selection is much longer than most of the selections in the *I Need The Light!* devotional book. In addition to its length, it has a different vibe than the other devotionals in the book. We know from the "Setting the Stage" section of the devotional that this is a letter Paul wrote to the church members at Corinth. We also know that the relationship between Paul and the Corinthian Christians was not good when he wrote the letter. Some of them had spoken out against Paul, but he was encouraging in his letter. He told them not to give up. How often have you felt like giving up? Did the words of Jesus or the words of Paul encourage you to keep trying? (I'm giving you extra space to write down your thoughts, because I have felt like giving up countless times. Living with several chronic illnesses has pushed me to my limit many times.)

Did the vivid imagery in *The Message* this week get your attention?

Do you think Paul's letter got the Corinthians' attention?

What is your favorite part of this week's Scripture, or what jumped out at you?

As written in *The Good News Bible*, this week's Scripture serves as a good reminder of how we should conduct our lives as Christians. We need to remember that we are merely clay pots and it is the power and glory that belong to God. Have you made any notes from this week's Scripture to remind yourself of Paul's words?

The last verse in II Corinthians 4:1-6, states in a nutshell what we are and who God is by comparison. The Light from God is a "precious treasure." It shines in each of us within our perishable bodies. Our bodies are weak and have limitations. The Light comes from God. The power and the glory are God's. Write any thoughts you have about that.

In *The Letters to the Corinthians, Revised Edition*, William Barclay pointed out that Paul was talking about four people or four sets of people. I must admit, I didn't catch on to that. Perhaps I did not study the Scripture deeply enough, or maybe my mind does not work like Rev. Barclay's trained theological mind. It is worth considering what Barclay said. What I liked best of Barclay's remarks was when he said "that in Jesus Christ we see what God is like." I find that incredibly reassuring! Now that you know Jesus, when you think of God, is that the way you see Him?

Do you see yourself as a messenger or errand runner for Jesus?

Do you know someone who would benefit from reading this devotional?

Did you smile about something every day this week?
Sunday

Monday

Tuesday

Wednesday

Thursday

Friday

Saturday

Did you buy yourself a box of chocolates this week "just because"?
If not a box of chocolates, did you buy yourself a different treat just
because you are you and you deserve it?

This week's comfort food recipe is for Fish Stew. Did you get to
make it and share it with someone?

Notes:

We Don't Belong to the Darkness

The Scripture for this week is I Thessalonians 5:5.

In the fourth chapter of I Thessalonians, Paul assured the people in the church at Thessalonica in Macedonia (present-day Greece) that if they believed in Jesus Christ, they would spend eternity in heaven. They were worried about the second coming of Christ and did not want to be taken unaware. They did not want to be taken off guard and surprised when Christ returned.

In this week's short Scripture, Paul reminded the Thessalonians that their future in the afterlife was already settled. He told them they were living in "the light" as opposed to "the dark," so they had nothing to worry about. That message is for us, too, as believers in Jesus Christ. Are you living in the certainty of spending eternity in heaven? Do you take comfort in Paul's words in I Thessalonians 5:5?

If doubts about where your soul is going when you die ever creep into your thinking, what do you do to combat those thoughts?

Are there other Bible versions besides I Thessalonians 5:5 that you can call to mind or find today that you can read or commit to memory the next time you wonder if you are going to heaven? If this is something that bothers you, take time to look for other assurances in the New Testament. Write them down.

Until you read the commentary by William Barclay in *The Letters to the Philippians, Colossians, and Thessalonians, Revised Edition* as presented in the devotional book, did you know about the Jewish belief in the Day of the Lord? It was a belief that the Christians at Thessalonica had grown up with — that the present age was all bad, then there would be a terrible Day of the Lord followed by the golden age of God. Their upbringing had trained them to fear the Day of the Lord. No wonder Paul was having to remind them that they had nothing to fear. Do you ever fear death or the Second Coming of Jesus, in case He returns while you are still alive? If so, reread Paul's letter to the Thessalonians. Take heart! Jesus does not want you living in fear.

In many aspects of my life, I am what one would call "a perfectionist." It is an enigma, but I know I cannot attain perfection. I want everything I do to turn out perfectly, although I know that is impossible. I get upset when things go wrong and don't turn out the way I would like. I guess that's why I included this week's Thought Pattern Interrupter in the devotional book. I need it for myself, and I need it every day. Has this week's Thought Pattern Interrupter helped you?

As winter is winding down, have you planned a day trip for the first warm day of the season? If you are able to travel, stop now and think about somewhere you'd like to go when the weather permits. If you are unable to travel, look at the listings on PBS on television and find a travel, cooking, or other show to watch that will transport you to another place for a few minutes or perhaps an hour or two.

Did you make Cherry Crisp this week? Consider putting a can of cherry pie filling and the other ingredients on your next grocery list.

Notes:

Brought Life and Immortality to Light Through the Gospel

T he Scripture for this week is II Timothy 1:10.

I think it helps to know Paul's circumstances at the time he wrote this letter to Timothy. Does knowing that Paul wrote this letter to Timothy from a prison cell as he awaited execution give his words in II Timothy 1:10 added weight and depth of meaning?

Few of us today face persecution for being Christians, so it is difficult to imagine Paul's circumstances. However, perhaps you work in
an office in which showing any outward signs that you are a Christian
is prohibited or brings on a co-worker's ridicule. How do you handle
that? Or, if it has not happened to you, how do you suppose you
would handle the situation?

Do you find comfort in Paul's admonishment that we should not
be ashamed to bear witness to Jesus Christ and accept any suffering we
might experience for doing so?

Knowing from William Barclay's commentary in *The Letters to
Timothy, Titus, and Philemon, Revised Edition*, that Paul was writing
Timothy in a time when the Stoics' belief that God gave people the
power to take their own lives help you to better understand what
might have prompted Paul to write II Timothy 1:10?

Have you experienced a level of fatigue or sickness in which you thought you were not going to be able to get well or keep going? If this is a chronic or constant situation for you, what makes you keep going?

Are you allowing yourself to look forward to spring?

Did you take time this week to evaluate your health and potential adjustments you need to make in your eating or exercise habits in preparation for a, hopefully, more active season ahead?

Do you know someone who might benefit from reading this devotional?

Did you make Joan's Chicken Pie? Will you make it again? Did you freeze some of it to enjoy at a later date?

Notes:

Chosen People... Out of Darkness into a Wonderful Light

T he Scripture for this week is I Peter 2:9-10.

In I Peter 2:9-10, we find Peter writing a letter of encouragement to the churches in Asia Minor, which is present-day Turkey. Knowing it was during the time of Nero's persecution of Christians around Rome adds a level of urgency to the letter. We talked about the persecution of Christians in Week 19, and I commented that I have never experienced persecution because I'm a Christian. Some people in the United States say they are being persecuted for their faith, but when we consider the level of persecution in other countries and the level of persecution in the early centuries after Jesus Christ's crucifixion, I think the Christians in the United States today need to dial back their language.

Nero delighted in pitting Christians against dogs and other ani-
mals. He liked to burn Christians alive, often after having them covered in tar or pitch and tied to stakes. He even used their burning
bodies to light up his gardens.

Whatever discomfort Americans are experiencing for being Christians today pales in comparison to other times and other places. Have
you ever been persecuted for being a Christian?

I Peter 2:9-10 tells the Christians in Asia Minor that they were
chosen by God to do His work. What is God calling you to do?

This week's Scripture in *The Message,* uses the wording
"night-and-day difference" God had made for the letter's recipients.
The Living Bible and the *TouchPoint Bible* speak of God calling the
letter's recipients "out of the darkness into his wonderful light." The
New Revised Standard Version similarly refers to God calling them
"out of a darkness and into his marvelous light." Going along with
the theme of the devotional book and this companion journal and
diary, think about how God is calling you to come into His light. Write
about that.

Is God also prompting you to get some sunlight? It just might lift your spirits as well as providing your body with some much-needed Vitamin D.

Did anything in particular jump out at you in one or more of the versions of I Peter 2:9-10 as found in the devotional book?

Verse 10 is about God's mercy, going "from nothing to something, from rejected to accepted," God's kindness, and "Once you were not a people; now you are the people of God. Once you received none of God's mercy; now you have received his mercy." That's strong language. How do you think it made the recipients of the letter feel to hear those words? Read those words aloud to yourself and let them sink in. Those words are meant for you and me. Hold onto those words this week. Any thoughts?

I like the quote from William Barclay's book, *The Letters of James and Peter, Revised Edition*, that I quoted in the devotional book: "A very ordinary thing acquires a new value, if it has been possessed by some famous person.... It is so with the Christian. The Christian may be a very ordinary person but he acquires a new value because he belongs to God."

I don't own anything that belonged to a famous person, but I have my grandmother's treadle sewing machine that was manufactured around 1899 or 1900. If I had that sewing machine but had no idea where it came from or who it had belonged to, it would make a nice piece of furniture. However, knowing that my grandmother used that machine to make clothing for my father and his four siblings makes it more than a nice piece of furniture. Having that sewing machine makes me feel a tactile connection with my grandmother even though she died 23 years before I was born.

Can you identify with my example? Do you have something that belonged to one of your ancestors? Do younger members of your family know about it, so it won't just be tossed out sometime in the future? Take time to write down the significance of that item and its history. If no one is interested today, perhaps they will appreciate it later. If nothing else, put the piece of paper you write that explanation on in a drawer in that piece of furniture or tape it to the back or bottom of the item so they will find it later.

How does it make you feel in light of Barclay's explanation to know that you have value because you belong to God?

Sometimes we have negative feelings about how we look. Sometimes we are body shamed. How has this week's Thought Pattern Interrupter helped you?

Do you know someone who might benefit from reading this devotional?

Did you get the chance to do this week's activity suggestion? How did that go?

This week's recipe for Slow Cooker Hamburger and Barley Soup is perhaps my all-time favorite soup. Have you made it? Will you make it again? Did you freeze some for later?

Notes:

Every Perfect Gift...
From the Father of
Light and lights

T he Scripture for this week is James 1:16-17

One year probably in the 1980s or 1990s, the Presbyterian Women's (PW) Bible study was based on the Book of James. It was one of the most uplifting and easily understood studies the Presbyterian Church (USA) had for us when I was active in PW. My health is not conducive to my participation now, but I still recall our study of James. James had a heart for the poor and suffering people and emphasized a Christian's obligation to take care of them. What were your first thoughts when you saw that this week's Scripture was from the Book of James? What do you associate the Book of James with?

This week's two verses from the first chapter of James serve as a warning and a reassurance. I take it more as a reassurance. How does it strike you? As a warning or as a reassurance? Or both?

James 1:16-17 reminds us that all good gifts come from God. Is that how you think about God?

These verses remind us that God is the Creator of all light and that He shines forever. There is no change or shadow in God's light. If there were changes or variations of light in God, we would not be able to count on Him. What are your thoughts about the steadfastness of God — how you can always count on Him to be there for you?

As William Barclay points out in *The Letters of James and Peter, Revised*, James is stressing "The unchangeableness of God." Even though He created the sun, moon, and stars, they vary in the light they give, "but he who created them never changes." There are few things in life in which we can depend to never change. Name any that you can think of.

Do you know someone who might benefit from reading this devotional?

Has this week's Thought Pattern Interrupter helped you?

Did you get to make Easy Chicken Noodle Soup this week? Were you able to share it with someone? It's hard to beat a chicken soup!

Notes:

If We Walk in Light,... Christ... Cleans Us from All Sin

T he Scripture for this week is I John 1:5.

In the "Setting the Stage" section of Week 25 in the devotional book, I commented that I John 1:5 "is so simple, yet profound, that its wording is almost identical in every version of the Bible that I read." It is a concise one-sentence statement of what God is: "God is light, pure light; there's not a trace of darkness in him." With an understanding of the light of God being pure and nothing but good, this statement tells us just about all we need to know about God. There is nothing but goodness in God so, if we believe in and worship God, how can it help but reflect in our lives?

In *The Letters of John and Jude, Revised Edition*, William Barclay states, "A man's character will necessarily be determined by the character of the god whom he worships;...." I had never thought about that, but it makes sense. Was this a new perspective for you to consider?

Barclay points out that darkness is the opposite of the Christian life throughout the New Testament. He reminds us that darkness will never overcome the light. He goes on to refer to the fruits of the Holy Spirit: love, joy, peace, longsuffering, gentleness, goodness, faith, meekness, and temperance. None of those attributes will grow in the absence of the Light of Jesus Christ. Darkness is life separated from God. Think about your experience with gardening, farming, or simply having a single potted plant in your home. Think about the importance of sunlight to the health — the very survival — of all those plants. It is the same for you and me. Even people who deny the existence of God cannot live without the light and goodness of God. Without God, there is no life. What are your thoughts?

"Spring is coming!" I hope this week's Thought Pattern Interrupter is giving you hope and comfort this week!

Did you get an opportunity to call a Ronald McDonald House or similar facility to ask what they need? How did it go? Is this something you want to do again?

Did you make Double Fudge Pudding? Were you tempted to eat it all in one sitting? Don't laugh! When I was in my twenties, living by myself, and not worried about gaining weight, on more than one occasion I made this recipe on Friday night and by Sunday night I had eaten the entire thing! Needless to say, I cannot do that now, and I'm not proud of doing it 45 years ago. I was allergic to chocolate until I was 16 years old so, in my twenties, I was trying to make up for lost time. I hope you enjoy this recipe!

Notes:

God is Light

T he Scripture for this week is I John 1:6-10.

Congratulations! You have made it to Week 26 in our journey through fall and winter! There is light at the end of the tunnel. (Pardon the light pun!)

This week's devotional picked up where Week 25 left off. Take a moment to reread I John 1:5, if you wish, and then continue reading through verse 10. Read those verses slowly. Read them aloud if you wish or are in a space where you can do that. There is a lot to digest in I John 1:6-10. It is a warning. I thought long and hard about which "light" or "The Light" Scripture to use for the last week in the devotional book. We don't just need Jesus Christ — The Light of the World" — in the fall and winter. We need Him every day of our lives, so I settled on these five Bible verses to share this week for you to carry with you throughout the spring and summer. What are your thoughts about that?

What jumped out at you as your read I John 1:6-10?

Which of the five versions of the Bible quoted in the devotional book this week spoke to you?

Variations of the word "lie" are found in this week's Scripture. We tend to think of a lie as something that is said or put in writing that is not true, but in this Scripture, John warns us in no uncertain words that if we say we have fellowship with God but continue to live in darkness, we are lying. I dare say, if we think we are in fellowship with God while we continue to live in a way that we know is in conflict with the will of God and the teachings of Jesus Christ, we are lying. Your thoughts? Had you ever thought of that as lying?

I struggle with anger management. Are you living lie in any aspect of your life?

This week's Scripture goes on to remind us that God is ready to forgive us if we only confess our sins to Him. I fall short of doing God's will every day, but I am able to move forward knowing that God listens to my prayers and He forgives me of those sins I confess. Sometimes doubts fill our minds and we think that maybe we have done or said something so bad that God will not or cannot forgive us, but that's not what I John 1:6-10 says. Do you ever have doubts about God's willingness to forgive you?

In *The Letters of John and Jude, Revised Edition*, William Barclay tells us that when I John was written, there were people who thought they were too intellectual and spiritual to be subject to laws or the idea of sin. That wasn't just true 2000 years ago! That is still true today. Have you ever known someone who thought they were too smart to believe in God?

Do you know someone who might benefit from reading this devotional?

What does this week's Thought Pattern Interrupter mean to you? If it were spring year round every year, would you take spring for granted? Would you get bored with it always being spring?

Have you taken time to do this week's suggested activity? I dare you!

Did you make Marie's Macaroni and Chicken Casserole? Comforting, isn't it?

Notes:

My Prayer for You

Now that you have made it through another autumn and winter, my prayer is that you are feeling refreshed and renewed. I pray that you are now welcoming spring and summer and perhaps a lessening of your aches and pains. I pray that the Scriptures highlighted in this devotional book and the companion journal/diary have lightened your load and equipped you to face next autumn and winter with less dread and anxiety than you have in the past.

I pray that, even though the aches and pains of chronic illness might ebb and flow, you will find peace and not let your unease about the coming winter prevent you from enjoying the beauty of autumn.

I pray that you will be able to adopt my mother's often-said words to live by: Take one day at a time. That is easier said than done. I know, because I have been trying to practice that all my life. It does us no good to let tomorrow ruin today. It is not good to let our anticipation of the cold days of winter ruin the crisp and colorful days of autumn. In most of the world God has blessed us with four distinct seasons. He wants us to find joy in each of them. I pray that you will seek the support of

God the Father, God the Son, and God the Holy Spirit every day of your life. Seek God's will, accept His forgiveness and grace, and let His Light shine through you in every season of the year and every season of your life.

I pray that you have everything you need and that you live in a place of contentment. I pray that the words of Paul in the eighth chapter of Romans will give you peace.

Romans 8:38-39, as written in *The Message*: "I'm absolutely convinced that nothing — nothing living or dead, angelic or demonic, today or tomorrow, high or low, thinkable or unthinkable — absolutely nothing can get between us and God's love because of the way that Jesus our Master has embraced us."

Romans 8:38-39, as written in *The Good News Bible*: "For I am certain that nothing can separate us from his love: neither death nor life, neither angels nor other heavenly rulers or powers, neither the present nor the future, neither the world above nor the world below — there is nothing in all creation that will ever be able to separate us from the love of God which is ours through Christ Jesus our Lord."

Romans 8:38-39, as written in The Living Bible: "For I am convinced that nothing can ever separate us from his love. Death can't, and life can't. The angels won't, and all the powers of hell itself cannot keep God's love away. Our fears for today, our worries about tomorrow, or where we are — high above the sky, or in the deepest ocean — nothing will ever be able to separate us from the love of God demonstrated by our Lord Jesus Christ when he died for us."

Romans 8:38-39, as written in The New Oxford Annotated Bible (NRSV): "For I am convinced that neither death, nor life, nor angels, nor rulers, nor things present, nor things to come, nor powers, nor height, nor depth, nor anything else in all creation, will be able to separate us from the love of God in Christ Jesus our Lord."

Romans 8:38-39, as written in TouchPoint Bible: "And I am convinced that nothing can ever separate us from his love. Death can't, and life can't. Our fears for today, our worries about tomorrow, and even the powers of hell can't keep God's love away. Whether we are high above the sky or in the deepest ocean, nothing in all creation will ever be able to separate us from the love of God that is revealed in Christ Jesus our Lord."

Remember: Nothing can separate you from the love of God.

About the author

J anet Morrison grew up in Harrisburg, North Carolina. She holds a Bachelor of Arts degree in Political Science with a minor in History from Appalachian State University and a Master of Public Affairs from North Carolina State University at Raleigh. In 2001, Janet took a fiction writing course at Queens University of Charlotte. It was a life-changing course. She is a lifelong Presbyterian and comes from a long line of Presbyterians and Methodists.

Janet wrote this devotional book out of her decades of experience with Chronic Fatigue Syndrome, Fibromyalgia, and Seasonal Affective Disorder. She needs natural light in the mornings to combat Seasonal Affective Disorder, and she needs Jesus Christ — The Light of the World — to cope with all life's challenges and stresses.

In her blog, Janet's Writing Blog, Janet writes opinion pieces about current events, shares her thoughts about some of the books she reads, writes posts of historical significance on or near the anniversary dates of those events, and occasionally writes about local North Carolina history. Find her blog at https://www.janetswritingblog.com.

Her website is https://www.janetmorrisonbooks.com By visiting her website, you can subscribe to her newsletter.

Here is the QR Code for your convenience:

Also by Janet Morrison

I f you are using or considering using this *I Need The Light! Companion Journal and Diary*, you are no doubt familiar with *I Need The Light! 26 Weekly Devotionals to Help You Through Winter*. That devotional book was Janet Morrison's first attempt to write a devotional book. Shortly after its publication, she had the idea to create this companion journal and diary.

Janet recommends that you use this journal alongside the devotional book because the devotional book contains the weekly Scriptures quoted from five different versions of the Bible, her thoughts, commentary, a sentence to remember each week, a Thought Pattern Interrupter, an Activity Suggestion, and a weekly comfort food recipe.

As a freelance writer, Janet wrote a local history column for *Harrisburg Horizons* newspaper in Harrisburg, North Carolina, from May 2006 through 2012. In 2022 and early 2023, she published those newspaper articles in paperback and e-book with the titles *Harris-*

burg, Did You Know? Cabarrus History, Book 1 and *Harrisburg, Did You Know? Cabarrus History, Book 2.* Those books are available in paperback at Second Look Books in Harrisburg, NC and available in paperback and e-book from Amazon.

Two of her historical short stories, "Slip Sliding Away: A Southern Historical Short Story" and "Ghost of the Battle of Guilford Courthouse: An American Revolutionary War Ghost Story," were published as stand alone stories and are available in paperback and e-book from Amazon. They will be included in Janet's upcoming book, *Traveling Through History: A Collection of Historical Short Stories*, along with a variety of short stories that will transport you from Scotland in the 1600s to Colonial times in America to the late 20th century. She plans to publish the short story collection in the fall of 2025.

Her vintage postcard book, *The Blue Ridge Mountains of North Carolina*, was published in 2014 by Arcadia Publishing. It is available in paperback and e-book from Amazon and in paperback from Arcadia Publishing. It is occasionally available at independent bookstores in western North Carolina, or you can request that your favorite bookstore order it for you.

Janet and her sister, Marie Morrison, published a family cookbook in 2023. The title is a play on words that came from a multi-generational tradition in their family. *The Aunts in the Kitchen: Southern Family Recipes* contains recipes from all the aunts in their family. Janet and Marie are now affectionately known as "The Aunts" by their nieces and nephews. It is a moniker they claim with pride. The cookbook includes snippets of information and memories of Janet and Marie's aunts. They were all good cooks! The cookbook is available in paperback at Second Look Books in Harrisburg, NC and from Amazon.

In 1996, Janet and Marie, compiled and published three genealogy books: *Descendants of John & Mary Morrison of Rocky River*, *Descendants of James & Jennet Morrison of Rocky River*, and *Descendants of Robert & Sarah Morrison of Rocky River*. Those hardback books are available through https://www.janetmorrrisonbooks.com.

Janet is writing an historical novel set along the Great Wagon Road in Virginia, North Carolina, and South Carolina in the 1760s.

She thanks you for purchasing this devotional book companion journal and diary and hopes it will bring you peace. If you are so inclined, she would appreciate your rating or even leaving a short review of this and her other books on Amazon, Goodreads, or other online review venues. Reviews are incredibly valuable to writers, especially when they, like Janet, are trying to establish credibility and name recognition. Thank you for purchasing, reading, reviewing, and telling your friends about this book!

For book descriptions and purchasing information, visit Janet's website: https://www.janetmorrisonbooks.com. Here is a QR code for your convenience:

Thank you for purchasing *I Need The Light! Companion Journal and Diary*. Please rate the book on Goodreads, Amazon, and other places where you look for book reviews.

Janet's Parting Words for you

Remember: The Word of God is a lamp to your feet and light to your path.

Psalm 119:105, the Scripture from Week 2 in this devotional book, as written in *The New Oxford Annotated Bible (NRSV)*: "Your word is a lamp to my feet and a light to my path."

www.ingramcontent.com/pod-product-compliance
Lightning Source LLC
Chambersburg PA
CBHW071304130626

46556CB00003B/1461